Fur-Ever Grateful

A Mother's Day Coloring Book for Dog Moms

Dear dog mom,

As a devoted dog mom myself, I know firsthand the joy and unconditional love that our furry children bring to our lives. They're there for us through thick and thin, always eager to snuggle, play, and make us laugh.

That's why I'm thrilled to introduce you to 'Fur-Ever Grateful,' the ultimate Mother's Day coloring book for dog moms.

This book is a celebration of the special bond we share with our four-legged friends, filled with heartwarming illustrations of different breeds of dogs, each with their unique personality and charm.

With every stroke of your crayon, colored pencil, or marker, you'll immerse yourself in the beauty and love of the canine world, and create a personalized tribute to your furry child that celebrates the unique connection you share.

Whether you're looking for a relaxing way to unwind, a thoughtful gift for the dog mom in your life, or simply a way to express your love and gratitude for your furry friend, 'Fur-Ever Grateful' is a perfect choice.

So sit back, relax, and let your creativity flow – because with this coloring book, you're fur-ever grateful for the love and loyalty of your furry friend.

Happy coloring!